The Fireside Book

A picture and a poem
for every mood
chosen by

David Hope

Printed and Published by
D. C. THOMSON & CO., LTD.,
185 Fleet Street, London EC4A 2HS.
ISBN 0-85116-489-7

ON THE DOWNS

I WANT to be on the downland,
  By the restless, tossing sea,
Where the lark above is singing
  And the winds are racing free!
And there midst the windswept grasses,
  Is a place for you and me.

The gulls are mournfully crying
  And flapping far away;
Far out on the gleaming waters
  They ride through the surging spray;
Where the wave-crests shine in the sunlight,
  They float through the Summer day.

Then come, in the clear May morning,
  Away by the tossing sea;
The gorse is a golden glory,
  And it's there that I would be!
Where the strong, free winds are racing,
  And calling to you and me.

Iris M. Raikes

A CORNER OF THE GARDEN

IN a corner of the garden
   All the richest roses grew,
And you found a wealth of sweetness
   Which the world never knew.

Where the fountain flung its gemlights
   On the lawn and gay parterre,
I had sought you long and vainly,
   But I could not find you there.

Where your sisters smiled and beckoned
   From the terrace in the sun,
There were roses, many roses,
   But I missed the sweetest one.

Just a rustle in the ivy,
   Just a quiver in the green,
And a vision of white raiment
   Gleaming through the leafy screen.

And I found you in the shadows,
   With your bright hair dashed with dew,
In a corner of the garden
   Which no stranger ever knew.

Sarah Doudney

NOCTURNE

UNDER the great white moon, the tawny owl
   Floats through the dim immensity of sky,
While small stars, trembling, pierce the stilly void,
   And clouds, like silver wraiths, speed softly by.

Under the great white moon, the sleeping world
   Is hushed and breathless, while each pallid flower
Quivers, and folds her petals tighter yet,
   As midnight chimes . . . and comes the witching
      hour!

Kathleen O'Farrell

TRAVELLER'S TALE

JUST for a dare, the other day,
  I crossed a hot and arid plain,
To where Seville in splendour lay,
    Although I've never been to Spain.

Above a reef of turquoise cloud
    I pirouetted in the sky;
In ecstasy I laughed aloud,
    And yet I've never learned to fly.

Arm over arm in half an hour
    I swam the Channel, rim to rim;
And people marvelled at my power,
    But I confess I cannot swim.

I've sailed beyond the Golden Gate,
    And kissed a girl in Samarkand;
But why my train is always late
    I'm sure I'll never understand.

Peter Cliffe

RETIREMENT

HIS days of needful toil gone by,
    Unhurriedly he takes his walk,
Blessing the new-found time, now his,
To stop and talk;
To hear opinions, exchange views,
And say what should or should not be,
Putting the crazy world to rights—
His friends and he.

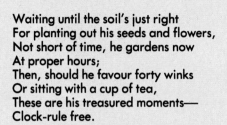

Waiting until the soil's just right
For planting out his seeds and flowers,
Not short of time, he gardens now
At proper hours;
Then, should he favour forty winks
Or sitting with a cup of tea,
These are his treasured moments—
Clock-rule free.

He'll don his waders, wind his reel
To fish within some quiet stream,
It matters not if there's no bite,
He can but dream.
He bowls the jack; he curls the stone
With well-aimed shot to cries of "Sweep";
Carefree, content he now, at eve,
Finds no more need for counting sheep!

Mary M. Milne.

WINTER SUNSET

TONIGHT, against the opal sky,
  The pinnacles of the peaks
Point ivory fingers to the stars;
  Westward the smouldering sunset reeks.

Carpets immaculate, shining snow,
  The hills that, like a stair,
Mount range on range and ridge on ridge,
  And melt into the shining air;

Where all the colours of the world
  Seem blended in one living glow,
That paints the sunset on the moors
  And on the shining snow.

Malcolm K. MacMillan

THE WIND AND THE SEA

OH, but if the wind would blow
   And bring the sound of the sea
To rustle in the green, green branches
   Of my tall apple tree,
I'd know the sound of the sunlit ripples
   Dancing along the sea.

And if the wind would blow again
   And bring the smell of the sea
To flicker in the rosy blossom
   Of my tall apple tree,
I'd know the smell of the rusty tangle
   Drifting upon the sea.

And if the wind would blow three times
   And bring the spray of the sea
Like dew upon the leaves to settle
   On my tall apple tree,
I'd lick my lips for the salty water
   Blown to me from the sea.

John Buxton

SOHO

CELERIAC and aubergine
    And glossy peppers red and green,
And Beaune and Riesling and Tokay
Shine in the shops as you pass by;
And in the streets the people go,
As black as grapes, as white as dough,
As golden as a honeycomb —
A thousand races, all at home.
And work and sloth and faith and fraud
And jolly sins that men applaud
And shabby ones they hope to hide
Are floating on that motley tide
That eddies where the nations meet
In Greek and Frith and Compton Street.
A thousand cooks, a thousand spices,
And hopes and fears and curious vices,
A thousand kinds of prayer and praise
And half a week of Sabbath days.
And though we be, as some have said,
Gomorrah, ripe for striking dead,
If we be spared, perhaps from them
May grow the New Jerusalem.

Audrey Field

MOVEMENT IN MAY

WIND ruffles the rain pools,
    Brisk clouds fuss across the sun
Sending wide sweeps of shade
Over green land to swallow up brightness
Then have it re-appear.
Crow-shadows flicker
Over the few furrows
Where growing is still a dark secret.
On the loose rope
Strung between trees
A mother's energetic arms
Hang out clothes from a red basket
And the wind, like gusty laughter,
Flings them in her face.

Margaret Gillies Brown

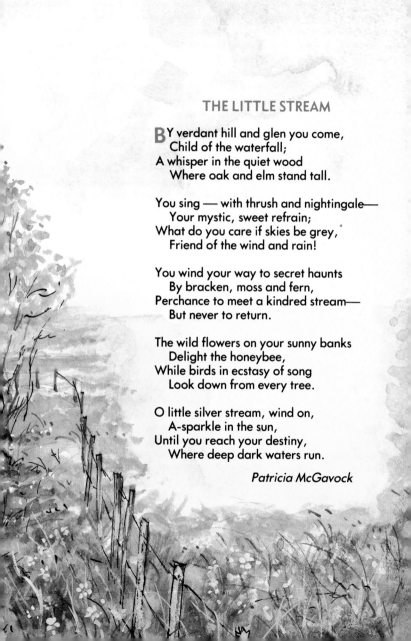

THE LITTLE STREAM

BY verdant hill and glen you come,
   Child of the waterfall;
A whisper in the quiet wood
   Where oak and elm stand tall.

You sing — with thrush and nightingale—
   Your mystic, sweet refrain;
What do you care if skies be grey,
   Friend of the wind and rain!

You wind your way to secret haunts
   By bracken, moss and fern,
Perchance to meet a kindred stream—
   But never to return.

The wild flowers on your sunny banks
   Delight the honeybee,
While birds in ecstasy of song
   Look down from every tree.

O little silver stream, wind on,
   A-sparkle in the sun,
Until you reach your destiny,
   Where deep dark waters run.

Patricia McGavock

OCTOBER REDBREAST

AUTUMN is weary, halt, and old;
    Ah, but she owns the song of joy!
Her colours fade, her woods are cold:
    Her singing-bird's a boy, a boy.

In lovely Spring the birds were bent
    On nests, on use, on love, forsooth!
Grown-up were they. This boy's content,
    For his is liberty, his is youth.

The musical striplings sings for play,
    Taking no thought, and virgin-glad.
For duty sang those mates in May.
    This singing-bird's a lad, a lad.

Alice Meynell

DREAMS OF HOME

DROWSY, country hamlet,
   Where time is held quite still,
A stony track-way leading down
A gently sloping hill
To a sheltered, wooded valley
Where winding pathways thread
Trees of lacy apple-green,
Azaleas pink and red,
Their canopies cascading,
Brushing banks of powder-blue,
A dappled haze of perfumed bells
As sunbeams trickle through.
Whispering leaves and song birds,
Scents drifting on the air . . .
Dreams of home and England
And loved ones waiting there.

Kathryn Garrod

A TINKER'S SONG

MY love and I are far apart,
    For since my life began,
There's but one thing that I've desired—
    To be a tinkerman.

My love, she put her hand in mine
    And said we should be wed;
But were I not a tinkerman,
    Then I were better dead.

My love, she cried; so hard she tried
    To make me settle down;
But tinkers are a travelling breed
    And I'll not live in town.

My love, she watched me ride away,
    'Midst jingling pot and pan;
And then, I think she rued the day
    She'd loved a tinkerman.

My love and I are far apart,
    For since my life began,
There's but one thing that I've desired—
    To be a tinkerman.

Greta Aspland.

THE ROVING SHOE

I DREAMED I was the Captain of a bonny little vessel,
The Roving Shoe we called her and we sailed across
the sea.
A merchant coaster hailed us and we turned about and
waited
For Messer Marco Polo had come to call on me.

"I've read of you in history," I said, and
made a curtsey.
He rubbed his chin and pulled his cheek
and took me by the hand.
"'Tis good," he said, "to meet you — I've
heard of your adventures,
I hear of all your travels from a friend in
Fairyland."
His coat was made of velvet with golden
braid and buttons.
I gave him bread and honey and a drink of
lemonade;
I introduced my sailors, trusty fairy
seamen,
I took him to the galley to see
our silks for trade.

He said, "I like the food here and I like your gallant
    sailors,
I like you, little Captain, and I like *The Roving Shoe*.
You're off to Vladivostok? Well, I may be of assistance,"
And Messer Marco Polo said, "I'll come along with you."
We put ashore at Hong Kong, at Hankow and at Pekin,
We sat and ate some mangoes underneath a nutmeg
    tree—
We called at many islands, at Sambok and at Naku,
And Messer Marco Polo came all the way with me.
We didn't reach Formosa or even Vladivostok,
For my nice dream ended suddenly, as nice dreams
    always do,
But I'm very glad I met him, Messer Marco Polo,
Though he turned into a pillow when we sank *The
    Roving Shoe*.

                Gloria Rawlinson

THE SHIELING

I HAVE a shieling in my mind —
  A secret place;
I turn to it whene'er the wind
  Brushes my face.

Its walls are fashioned out of time
  And memory;
Its floor is quickened with the lime
  Of poetry.

Before the ever-open door
 Red rowans nod;
The mellow sunlight on the floor
 Minds me of God.

Upon the crickets' hearth is room
 For only me:
No shadow lingers there, nor gloom
 Creeps stealthily.

My sunny house is free from care
 And sorrow's blight;
The peace I seek is ever there,
 Both day and night.

God grant that I may always find
 The slender key
That opes the shieling in my mind —
 And sets me free.

Sydney Bell

SUMMER AFTERNOON

SHADOWS grow longer now upon the grass,
    And very soon these Summer hours will pass.
Each moment of this most delightful day
I now meticulously lay away
As lace in lavender — my treasure store
Of memory when I sit here no more.
But when my need is such, I will recall
These roses trailing over mellow wall,
The thrush's fluty song, the bumble bee
Upon the clover, and white clouds blowing free;
The blackbird seeking food at the lawn's edge,
Sweet heady scent of flowering privet hedge.
All this timeless beauty I shall relive
Because one Summer's day had much to give.

Barbara Jemison

THE FAIRY THORNS

CHILDREN, dear children, listen well to me!
  Wherever you may wander, wherever you
  may be
By dawnlight or twilight; at even or at morn,
Oh never, never — never ever! — harm a fairy
  thorn!

On the lonely hillside or by the wishing well
The fairy thorns are standing: what secrets they
  could tell
Of dancing in the moonlight when all the world's
  asleep.
And from their darkened windows mere mortals
  dare not peep!

When the rounded raths are dark against the sky
The fairy thorns stand waiting the curlew's eerie cry;
Waiting for the laughter, the music in the air,
The sudden wind that whispers among the
  branches bare.

Never — no, never — should you hear *them* sing,
Linger by a fairy thorn inside a fairy ring!
Bless yourself at once, ere they spirit you away
From cosy home and kindred, for a year and for a
  day!

Children, dear children, listen well again!
Take no heed of tapping upon your window pane!
Anger not The Good Folk, in malice or with scorn:
And never, never — oh no, never! — harm a fairy
  thorn!

Sydney Bell

CAUTION

GOOD friends, when offered tempting bait,
　　Don't pounce . . . but pause and ruminate
On what dread fate may lie in wait
For those who haste not hesitate.
A point I now will illustrate:

Within a burn, in frothy spate,
A speckled beauty freely ate
Whatever morsel passed his pate.
But had it stopped to cogitate
On hooks and lines, its final fate
Had not been on a dinner plate!

Noel Scott

ON THE SEASHORE

A STRETCH of yellow sand,
    The vast Sound broad and blue;
Two lovers hand in hand,
    Two lovers, I and you.

Far peaks the Sound that gird,
    No cloud in all the sky;
Two lovers without word,
    Two lovers, you and I.

Above the old kirkyard
    With lovers two and two;
Some old and evil-starred,
    Some young as I and you.

No fleck on sky or sea,
    Soft airs that loiter by;
How sweet past words to be
    Two lovers, you and I.

How sweet past words, and lo!
    Two lovers fond and true
Know all heart needs to know;
    Two lovers, I and you.

Yet there the grim walls stand
    Where death's mute victims lie,
While we walk hand in hand,
    Two lovers, you and I.

Latimer McInnes

PRUNING

W OULD that my tangled apple tree
   Could somehow chance to look
More like the perfect specimen
   That figures in my book!

For if it did, 'twould easy prove
   To clip it where I'm told,
With spurs to carry fruit, and strong
   New wood replacing old.

Confound the book! Its bland advice
   Is close akin, I fear,
To telling a lost traveller,
   "You shouldn't start from here!"

George Darwall

OUR OWN HOUSE

WHEN we have our own house,
   What shall we keep there?
Let's have a jug of flowers
   At the turning of the stair.

We'll take a pot of fresh paint
   To window and to door,
And we'll let in a sunbeam
   To shine across the floor.

Let's have a brass door-knocker
   And keep it shining bright
As the welcome that we give to friends
   Who knock there, day or night.

We'll have a fire upon the hearth
   When Winter nights are cold,
And company to cheer and comfort
   Both the young and old.

Let's keep enough of everything
   To satisfy our need,
But not too much of anything —
   For that would just be greed.

Let's keep the promises we made
   When we were one-and-twenty,
And pray that our house always will
   Be filled with love a-plenty.

Trudie Morgan

IDLE THOUGHTS

THE ceaseless roar of traffic passing by
    Comes to me from the lighted street below,
A never-ending and relentless stream,
Sweeping all onward in its steady flow;
Like some great river, full of living things
Caught in the swirl, and swept upon their way;
All rushing to a goal within some time
Ne'er pausing, even with the close of day.

Down in the dimness of the busy street,
I watch the dazzle of the lights that gleam
Like stars, reflecting from the darkened road,
And glitter onward with the roaring stream.
While the true stars, that all forgotten shine
Pale in the murky heavens far away,
Are blotted from this surging pulse of life,
Nor pierce the city's glare with feeble ray.

Yet these same stars are watching silent hills
And forests, dark beneath a frosty sky;
As, chill, the Autumn evenings quietly close,
While, in the mists, the sunset glories die.
From the cold turquoise of a Winter's eve,
This hour, when the trees are darkly flung
Against the lingering light, the magic moon
Climbing serenely, mid the clouds is hung.

Iris M. Raikes

A QUESTION

WHO lives in the house where the rose crowds
    high
As the weathered thatch, and the white birds fly
Like the ebb and flow of drifting waves,
From the dim-lit cool of the cobwebbed eaves,
And the silence loves their hooded cry?

Who lives where the window boxes spill
Wild riot, and green lichens fill
The time-stained, ornamental urn
Where memories of orchid burn,
Pink campion and cathedral bell?

Who lives where tangled vine has claimed
The violet wall, and brier untamed,
The weather-beaten, broken gate,
And the silence makes you stand and wait,
By a wilderness of fragrance fanned?

Beyond the door, 'twixt house and wall
Enfolded in cobweb and creeper and all,
She sits, perhaps, in the golden days
With the sigh of the breeze and her memories,
Till shadows steal and night birds call.

Eileen Melrose

WHAT IS LOVE?

LOVE is. . .
    Giving: as the sun gives light;
  And roses, perfume; bountiful and free.
Love asks no recompense: it is a flight
    Of generous thought, given unreservedly.

Love never makes demands, nor begs returns,
    But seeks the best, forgiving any faults;
Love is a heat that glows but never burns,
    A flow of warm delight that never halts.

And if you ask:—
"Can such a passion be?"
I'll say . . . my heart holds such a love for thee!

Noel Scott

THE GREY LAND

IN the chill of a grey evening
   Of the grey November time,
How the grey hills heave
Against the grey sky!
How the grey shadows climb
On the hillside!
How the grey gulls cry
And wheel above the tide!
And the grey rocks so still
And waves that roll
Work a strange, strong will
With the human soul.
How can I, then, be free;
Or how can I understand
The spell that is over me
In the grey land?

Malcolm K. MacMillan

THE FIDDLE

WHEN I was young, I had no sense,
  I bought a fiddle for eighteenpence,
And the only tune that I could play,
  Was "Over The Hills and Far Away".

To learn another I had no care,
  For oh! it was a bonny air,
And all the wee things of the glen
  Came out and gathered round me then.

The furry folk that dwell in wood,
  Quitted their hushed green solitude,
Came round about me, unafraid,
  And skipped to the music that I made.

I hied me up on the lone hill road
  Where the Little Green People have their abode,
And fiddled to them on the ruined cairn
  Till they all came out from the rush and fern.

'Twas I was the Captain of that band
  That played with me in fairy land,
Till the moon leaned over the hills to stare,
  And see who fiddled the fairy air.

Fr-r-rip! — the furry folk turned and fled,
  And every bird to the thicket sped.
In a flash my fairy friends were gone,
  And fiddle and I were all alone.

I sold my fiddle to buy a drum,
  But never again did the fairies come,
And all the bliss of that happy day
  Is Over the Hills and Far Away.

Neil Munro

AUTUMN LEAVES

THEY dance against my window-pane,
 And frolic down the village lane,
Gather in heaps — now here, now there,
Prance and gallop everywhere;
The wind comes wildly sweeping by,
Snatching them up into the sky:
High above my chimney pot
They whirl, as if each had forgot
An Autumn leaf, because it's late,
Should be quite modest and sedate;
Undignified they are, and yet
Their loveliness I can't forget,
Mauve, yellow, orange, crimson, brown,
Glowing like fire they tumble down—
He who doubts God in unbelief,
Has never seen an Autumn leaf.

Margaret H. Dixon

YASMEEN

MY window is open wide
    And the light from my lonely room
Streams out, a mellow path
Of gold in the velvet gloom;
And the silver-studded stars
Bend down to the singing sea:
But ah, though I wait and wait:
She does not come to me!

My window is open wide,
And over the garden far
The scent of the jasmine comes
Like light from a distant star.
And the crimson blossom falls
From the Bougainvillea tree:
But ah, though I wait and wait:
She does not come to me.

The murmur of violins
Lies warm on the scented air:
The gleam of her rounded arms!
The perfume of her hair!
Alone in the violet night,
My love goes winging free:
But ah! Though I wait and wait:
She does not come to me.

Sydney Bell

THE OLD FARM

THERE is a mellow stillness in the air
    Where the slow centuries have set their seal.
Though life is no more simple than elsewhere,
Forgotten loves are strong to soothe and heal
In ancient walls that have endured the rain
And stored the sun and sheltered death and birth
And welcomed back to the laggard Spring again
So many seasons to the greening earth.

So many years beloved, this quiet land
Achieves fulfilment, and a kind of bloom,
Like conkers fondled in a childish hand,
Or ancient wood, that in some homely room
Glows with the care that generations give
Who by long living learn at last to live.

Audrey Field

BON VOYAGE

THE sun is setting in the sea,
  The long bright day is o'er;
The night with all its mystery,
  Falls on the lonely shore.

The stars peep out, the night winds sigh
  Over both sea and land,
The rippling wavelets curl and die
  Upon the pebbled strand.

A tall ship ploughs its lonely way
  Across the darkening sea,
With twilight's last departing ray
  To keep her company.

So, bon voyage to you, stout barque,
  Farewell, old ship o' mine.
Goodbye, and God speed through the dark
  And southward o'er the Line.

And may no tempests wildly blow
  Or billows rage amain
To scourge the seas where'er you go
  Till you come back again.

C. W. Wade

PUFFING BILLY

IN youth's bright heyday, long ago, my little
  friends and I
Would sit upon the garden fence, to watch the
    trains go by,
And when we glimpsed a plume of smoke, we'd
    cheer with might and main,
As though to welcome all aboard our splendid
    "bonfire" train.

We'd see it coming from afar, so small, so trim and
    neat,
Chugging through the countryside, with steady,
    rhythmic beat,
And how excitedly we waved, as nearer still it
    came,
So mighty, so magnificent, its cabin lit with flame!

Oh, Puffing Billy, how our ears were deafened as
    you flew
Between the steep embankments where a million
    daisies grew,
Big, snowy daisies, golden-eyed . . . I see them
    shining yet,
They symbolise those halcyon days I never will
    forget.

We had such simple pleasures then, and none of us
    could boast
Of travelling any farther than the Kent or Sussex
    coast,
But in our dreams we journeyed far, cross land, and
    sea, and sky;
No wonder that our pulses raced, when Billy
    thundered by!

Kathleen O'Farrell

THE PEAT-STACK

THE brown and comforting peat-stacks have
   stood,
  Fire's fuel for my Hebridean home,
Cut, where some proud and prehistoric wood
  Lies levelled to the land in peaty loam.

Through damp December's mirky, moonless eves,
  The ceilidh's lore goes round, and firelight
   mellows
The hardiest sceptic till he half-believes.
  The wheezing of the old, asthmatic bellows
Stirs up the blaze; and through the open thatch
  The fiery stars fly skyward in the storm,
Inviting travellers at the friendly latch
  To come within the peat-fire's circle warm;
While on its heart the fire builds memories
  Of tropic forests in the Hebrides.

Malcolm K. MacMillan

CORNFIELDS

CORNFIELDS under a crescent moon
  Swung aloft in the midnight sky;
Restless feet of the straying wind
Rustling onward, passing by
Into the woodland shadows dim,
  Where the owls are calling.

Cornfields under the August sun;
Gathered harvest, in stooks of gold,
Vanished haven of fox and hare;
Nothing left save the stubble, cold.
Into the covert wild things fly,
    When the sheaves are falling.

Stubble-fields in the early dew;
Jewels sparkle on every thorn;
Mist is hiding the silent hill.
Waken echoes! Awake, the horn!
Fox-cubs fly, for your hour is come
    When the leaves are falling.

Iris M. Raikes

TWILIGHT

IT is evening, and the sun has set
   Over the hills, and the cherry tree,
Over the town with its shops and streets,
Over the lights, that shine back at me,
And all the work of the busy day
Is now discarded, and put away.

It is twilight, and the little stars
Light up the sky with their gentle glow,
A time that is soft, and still and sweet,
A pause in the frenzied world we know,
When I can sit 'neath my own rooftree,
And let the dusk encompass me.

If I could choose that time stand still,
At a moment more special that all the rest,
If I could stop it, at my own will,
To be my own — and my very best,
It would be the hour — not day — not night,
But the space between — the dear twilight.

Margaret H. Dixon

ON THE RIVER

O SWEET Spring days!
   Upon the shining reaches of the river,
When April dances down the flowery ways
Above the fens where scented breezes shiver:
O sweet Spring days!

Dream-golden days!
When on soft banks faint hawthorns pale and quiver
And drowsy sweet, the slow bough softly sways
Above the silent reaches of the river:
Dream-golden days!

Dear far-off days!
Adown the rippling reaches of the river,
Deep in my wandering heart their sweetness stays:
Ah! fade ye may, but ye can leave me never,
Dear far-off days!

Through golden days
Could we, adown the reaches of life's river,
Glide on, dear love, to parting of the ways,
Then kiss farewell — and meet to see for ever
Heaven's golden days!

Herbert Kennedy

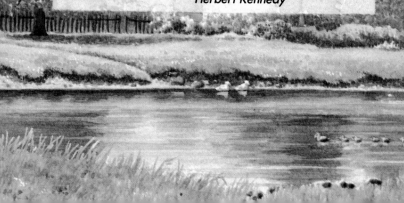

VINNIE

YOU filled my heart with laughter,
    Or else my eyes with tears.
How memories, like music,
    Come dancing down the years!

Your hair was brown as Autumn;
    Your eyes as blue as Spring;
Your voice had all the sweetness
    Of Summer larks a-wing.

You teased me without mercy,
    And swore I'd not be true.
Oh, Vinnie, in your girlhood
    None was as cruel as you!

One day I spoke in anger
    And turned to walk away;
Ah, then you said you loved me
    And told me I must stay.

The sun beamed warm approval:
    How bright it seemed to shine!
With love and tears and laughter
    I took your hand in mine . . .

Peter Cliffe

THE MOAT

AROUND this lichened home of hoary peace,
  Invulnerable in its glassy moat,
A breath of ghostly Summers seems to float
And murmur mid the immemorial trees.
The tender slopes, where cattle browse at ease,
Swell softly, like a pigeon's emerald throat:
And, self-oblivious, Time forgets to note
The flight of velvet-footed centuries.

The golden sunshine, netted in the close,
Sleeps indolently by the yew's slow shade;
Still, as some relic an old master made,
The jewelled peacock's rich enamel glows;
And on yon mossy wall that youthful rose
Blooms like a rose which never means to fade.

Mathilde Blind

AFTER RETIRAL

WHEN I left the old office behind me,
  I skipped down the stairs like a boy;
I laughed and I joked, and very near choked,
  And my face was just beaming with joy.
To do something big and important,
  I swore — in the height of my glee.
But after three years, I'm a bit in arrears,
  For this is what happens to me:

*On Monday I feel tired and languid,
  On Tuesday I feel just the same;
When Wednesday comes, I meet all my chums,
  On Thursday the weather's to blame.
Friday is nearly the end of the week,
  It's no good of starting then;
So I lay down my head, on the old feathered bed,
  Till Monday comes round again.*

I'm full of the best of intentions,
　　But something will come in the way;
The spirit is willing and eager,
　　But the flesh seems to jib at the fray.
I dream, and I scheme, of some action,
　　That will fill the whole country with bliss;
And I swear, with a prayer, I will yet manage there,
　　If things didn't happen like this:

On Monday I feel tired and languid,
　　On Tuesday I feel just the same;
When Wednesday comes, I meet all my chums,
　　On Thursday the weather's to blame.
Friday is nearly the end of the week,
　　It's no good of starting then;
So I lay down my head, on the old feathered bed,
　　Till Monday comes round again.

William Neish

PLOUGHING SONG

TIS up we are wi' the risin' sun
  To a fresh wind blowin' free,
And out wi' a swingin' gait to plough
  Go Dandy, Bess and me;
And oh, tis grand i' the early morn
  When the lark trills high and clear,
And the clankin' whoosh o' the turnin' sod
  Is music to my ear.

Old Tom next door, wi' his iron horse,
  Roars clatterin' by all day,
And he laughs at Dandy, Bess and me
  As he leaves us ploddin' away:
But they're not for me these new-found ways
  O' tillin' and seedin' the land—
There's nowt beats the pride o' my sturdy pair
  And the feel o' the plough in my hand,

And the lapwing's peevish anxious cry
  Lest her eggs be trampled o'er,
The screamin' gulls and the curlew's call,
  Joys that Tom knows no more.
I'll grant he's fast wi' his modern gear,
  Yet his seeds grow along o' mine,
And I reap and gather along o' Tom
  When the harvest moon's a-shine.

Mary M. Milne

THOSE HATS!

WHEN I buy a hat I do observe convention;
   But women! Anything becomes a crown:
A lampshade; fruit; whatever they can wrench on,
   Is worn with proud parade around the town.

I wonder why they wear such strange creations?
   Extravagance? Or what? Please, ladies, tell us!
You don these hats to win men's admiration?
   Or just to make the other women jealous?

Thank goodness, I don't get these foolish fancies.
   But girls . . . they are that way, and ever will
     be.
New hats — new loves! Sweet souls, that's where
     romance is . . .
   But I'm content to buy the old brown trilby!

Noel Scott

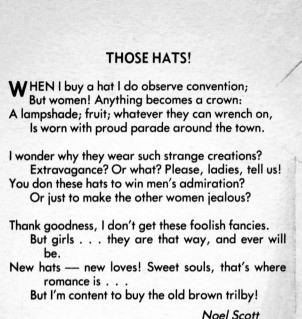

BEAUTY

IT is Beauty itself I seek — not beautiful things!
  The something that shivers the heart when a
    linnet sings;
That colours the gossamer web on the whin at
    dawn,
And skies — that are not of this world — when day
    has gone.

The blue of the distant hills brings joy to me
As the scarlet rowan, the froth of the blackthorn
    tree;
Or the peace of the wine-red moor where the
    curlew cries,
And the love that shines through the soul in a little
    dog's eyes!

This is the Beauty I seek and desire to hold,
Woven into my being with skein of gold:
Ethereal: lifting me up above earthly things
Till I soar to the foot of God's throne — on
    Beauty's wings!

Sydney Bell

GALLOPING ON

WHEN sunrise is lifting the curtain of dawn
    From the glistening hills, from the slumbering plain,
We are galloping into the magical day,
To capture it 'ere it shall vanish again.
So swiftly it passes, so swiftly it fades,
A mystery lighting the hills and the sky;
And over the threshold of morning alone,
We are galloping on, you and I.

The sunset is glowing afire in the west,
From a limitless sea, from the edge of the world.
We are galloping over the crest of the hill,
The valley below us is dimly unfurled;
Remote, in the shadows, with heaven so near,
And earth far away, but a dream that shall die;
Right into the heart of the sunset, alone,
We are galloping on, you and I.

When darkness has fallen around us at last,
And all our tomorrows have faded away,
We'll gallop alone in a shadowy land,
To find the lost light of the radiant day.
Perhaps we may capture a wonderful life,
Where glory will triumph, and youth cannot die;
And so to the end of our quest, little mare,
We'll be galloping on, you and I.

Iris M. Raikes

THE KILT'S MY DELIGHT

WOOL from the mountain, dyes from the vale,
    Loom in the clachan, peat-fires bright;
To every strand of it some old tale —
    Oh, the tartan kilt is my delight!
Went to its spinning brave songs of Lorn;
    Its hues from the berry and herb were spilt;
Lilts of the forest and glee of morn
    Are in his walking who wears the kilt!

For priest nor clerk nor merchant men,
    Nor biders at home was the pleating pressed,
But for the loins of those who ken
    Hill-wandering, offspring of the mist;
Wood-trackers, waders of wild streams,
    The world their pillow, their roof the night;
Who sleeps in tartan has high dreams,
    Oh, the kilt of the Highlands is my delight!

I will put on me that gallant gear,
    Brave first garb of the human kind,
Travel the moors and the hills of deer,
    And feel on my body the kiss of the wind.
Be it melting heat or the driven sleet,
    Kings to stand with or foes to fight,
Dance in the shieling, or death to meet,
    Oh, the darling kilt is my delight!

Neil Munro

GIFTS

HERE I come with gifts, my dear,
　　Pearls nor posies bringing,
But a net of gossamer
　　Full of sweetest singing.

Mavis trill and warbler's note,
　　Blackbird's rich out-pouring,
Priceless rapture from the throat
　　Of lark in blue skies soaring.

Last night 'neath the moon's clear sheen,
　　While the birds were sleeping,
Thro' a sea of coolest green
　　Softly I went creeping;

Gath'ring songs that all the day
    In the air are roaming,
But in clustered bubbles gay
    Fill the trees at gloaming.

Then at dawn I made a net,
    Silvery webs a-pleating,
Melodies all dewy yet
    To bear to you as greeting.

Hylda C. Cole

FACE IN THE CROWD

THIS man is other than he seems:
   His roots are in the long ago,
In barley-lands of yesterday;
And through his mind at sunset blow
The echoes of primeval dreams.

Though seedlings on his window-sill
Are all his little holding now,
And though he does not even know
What fields his fathers used to plough,
The yeoman is a yeoman still.

Beneath his wary weather-eye
And huge, unhurried country tread,
The grass might grow on Ludgate Hill,
And all the buried lanes ahead
With hawthorns greet his passing by.

Audrey Field

THE BROOK

THE shining brook ran wild and free;
  Its whispering song, "Come, come with me!"

Cascading down a hill we flew,
Midst gorse of spiky yellow hue,
Under a bridge, arched and steep,
Bubbling on by grazing sheep;
Ducking branches newly-gowned,
Leaping rocks and swirling round
Bracken banks with decked display
Of heather, plucked along the way,
Past lonely farms where lichen cleaved
To dry stone walls as on we weaved
Into meadows strewn with flowers,
Meandering in the sun-lit hours,
Until a curlew's plaintive cry
Rose to meet an evening sky.

Kathryn L. Garrod

THE MOLE CATCHER

HE comes by stealth in the morning
    And nobody sees him pass;
With never a moment's warning
    He's there on the dewy grass;
In an ancient hat all glairy
    He looks like a battered elf;
He's whiskered and wise and wary,
    And almost a mole himself.

There's scarcely a soul can name him,
    For simply "The Catcher" he;
But leagues of the Lowlands claim him,
    He's theirs for a trifling fee.
And a summons will bring him speeding
    In a puffing and paintless shay;
Yet long ere the world is heeding
    He's finished and far away.

But if you should waken early
    And meet him in talking mood,
You'll find that this creature surly
    Is wise in the ways of the wood.
There's never a mole can beat him,
    He's worth far more than he's paid,
And you ought to be proud to greet him,
    For he's the last of his trade.

glairy — muddy
shay — chaise

Averil Stewart

THE HOUSEWIFE'S SONG

I WILL not go to outer space:
    The farthest that the mind can see
Finds not the spirit's dwelling-place;
    It is not far enough for me.

I'll chop no logic with the storm,
    Nor beat the bitter wind in vain,
But build a fire to keep you warm
    When you take shelter from the rain.

And I'll not lose you, though you soar
    So proud above my simple rhyme:
I do not doubt that, as before,
    You will be home by supper time.

Audrey Field

THOUGHTS IN SEPARATION

WE never meet; yet we meet day by day
    Upon those hills of life, dim and immense —
The good we love, and sleep, our innocence.
O hills of life, high hills! And, higher than they,
Our guardian spirits meet at prayer and play.
Beyond pain, joy, and hope, and long suspense,
Above the summits of our souls, far hence,
An angel meets an angel on the way.

Beyond all good I ever believed of thee
Or thou of me, these always love and live.
And though I fail of thy ideal of me,
My angel falls not short. They greet each other.
Who knows, they may exchange the kiss we give,
Thou to thy crucifix, I to my mother.

Alice Meynell

PROCESSIONAL

I MUST be rising and I must be going
  On the roads of magic that stretch afar,
By the random rivers so finely flowing
  And under the restless star.
I must be roving on the roads of glory,
  So I'll up and shoe me with red-deer hide.
For youth must be learning the ancient story —
  Let the wearied oldsters bide.

Neil Munro

ACKNOWLEDGEMENTS

We wish to thank the following for the use of their poems: Peter Cliffe, Mary M. Milne, Audrey Field, Patricia McGavock, Kathryn L. Garrod, Sydney Bell, Barbara Jemison, Noel Scott, Trudie Morgan, Margaret H. Dixon, Margaret Gillies Brown, and Eileen Melrose.